Forgiving My Mother

Rachell Hathaway

Copyright © 2021 Rachelle Hathaway.

ISBN:-13 9798814487469

Front cover image and book design by Armmer Entertainment.

Originally printed by www.thebookpatch.com

First printing, 2017.

Kindle Direct Publishing Team,
Seattle Washington, United States of America

www.shelhathaway.com

My prayer is that this story inspires someone who may be

stagnate in their life due to various circumstances. Ultimately everyone has difficult choices to face, how we face them has a great deal to do with many situations we go through. I found freedom from hatred and hurt through choosing to forgive and love my mother the way God intended her to be loved…unconditionally and without judgment. I love you Momma!

I am no one traveling in a world which is not my own. I am lost in a downward spiral of darkness, I am alone. I no longer have the presence of who I used to be. The existence of no one is who I am. My words unheard, so thoughts unspoken shelter a weeping heart, carry a weary mind and a hopeless dream. I am running away from this reality. The torment of my fears take hold; please help me, help save me! Without knowing who I am I am nothing who is no one.

~Shel

Childhood Memories

My earliest memory of neglect is being of school age

(maybe kindergarten or first grade) knocking on the door of our apartment crying because I was trying to get inside to get dressed for school. I knocked because I'd slept over at my Aunt's after one of my mother's party nights that left her too hung over to answer the door. I hated to do that; opening the door to a memory that I fought very hard to suppress. I hated feeling like a victim of circumstance and unloved. As a young child growing up I held on to more of the bad memories than the good. In time the good memories were so shallow I could hardly recall them to mind. I was frequently ill with various allergies and respiratory issues when I was young. I'd blocked out the fact that my mother would take special care of my skin and bought alternative food products due to my restrictions. Now this is not a big deal considering what many people feel that a mother is supposed to do. I felt the same way, but in time I learned that a large majority of us humans don't do what we are "supposed" to. Why should my mother be held to a different standard? Why was it so hard for me to grade her on a curve? For the most part my mom raised me as a single parent. My father was present in my life but lived in a different state. As a child, I thought my daddy sat the moon and hung the stars. He was my heartbeat and I thought he was the best daddy in the whole world. My dad came to town almost every month when I was in elementary. We always did fun stuff that I never did with my mom. He wanted to know how things were going with me. When I played soccer in eighth grade I remember him being at a ton of my games and he didn't even live here. My mom only came to one that I ever remember. My daddy took pictures on the side of the field and made me feel special and important. My mom never cared to show any interest in what I was doing, she just didn't care. Those were the thoughts that I carried day in and day out. Now, as a grown ass woman, I view the scenario of the way I characterized my mother and father very differently. Fact: I would be smart mouthed to my mom almost daily. I was a "have to have the last word" kind of kid. You know, the "if someone just shoves a fist down her throat she will shut up," type of kid. Fact: until about 7th grade I was a dirty little raga muffin. I was nowhere near the child that any one would hope for. I didn't want to clean my room and until I was in third grade I didn't really want to bathe. These simple things that all parents experienced, my mom experienced every day with me. When I was sick and had to be taken care of in the middle of the night, my mom (not my dad) lost sleep that evening. My mom, as anyone who is a parent would understand, was worn. Once all the "have to" tasks are taken care of, there isn't much energy to do the "want to" stuff anymore. Not to take shine from my daddy, he was and still is pretty cool. However, when he came to town he came to his little princess. He didn't have to endure the non-bathing, filthy roomed brat that my mom had to beat the night before. He would be greeted by an anxious mom hating, daddy loving little bug. Now what do you do when you haven't had to deal with a snot nosed brat for 20 sum odd days? You come bearing gifts; you come ready to listen; you are anxious to please, that is reality. Now don't get me wrong I am in no way claiming that children that are brats deserve to be mistreated, I feel all children should be loved to the max. I'm simply stating that no matter how wonderful a parent you are, there may come a day where your child is not so wonderful. The reason a child may not be wonderful in a situation is simple: they are learning as they grow. Similarly, the parent is learning to adapt and deal with discipline for unacceptable behavior as it happens. So, while I critiqued my mother daily on every level, my father stayed under the radar of my criticism. Now it is apparent to me that he wasn't on my radar at all because I didn't live with him. It is much easier to be the super parent when you don't have to wash pee filled underwear! Oh, and I failed to mention that my father was an educator before I was born. His aptitude to deal with children was totally different than my mother's in general. That is life though; it's not always balanced according to what is fair and right. There is no public service announcement that says "ungrateful children, your parents sacrifice for you, so behave and just listen to what they say." My mother would literally give me the checks my dad sent to use how I chose. Her action of taking no money, reflected that she handled the day to day living expenses, which is no small task. That was reality that I took for granted as a child because it was simply how things were. I needed a nudge to remind me that while my mother was not and will never be perfect, she did the best that she knew to do. I was angry with life in general, and it was all based on my relationship with my mother. I couldn't accept advice from her because I felt that she couldn't possibly advise me on any level because I wanted to be totally different from her. I'd often recall many things she did and the many ways in which she made me feel unloved through the years although there was no positive benefit to this emotional review.

God when I am down and don't know which way to turn,

I call your name. Are you listening? Oh help me to know that your love is shown by your sacrifice. Lord I am weak and at times I take my eyes off thee. Please forgive me Lord I am reaching out to you. You have been the one I could talk to. You know everything; I am myself with you. Yet you love me, I don't know why but you do and you treat me like no one can. So, I thank you; for through my weakness you teach me to be strong. You encourage me when others laugh at me and you comfort me when no one will listen. I can cry to you and never be ashamed because you have made me with my flaws. You accept me into your arms and cradle me to sleep each night. With the blessings of my first breath each morning I thank you. Guide me through these troubled waters and because I refuse to tread sometimes Lord, anchor me that I might not drift out with the tide and fade away to sink in the oceans' foam.

~Shel

My Circumstances

There were so many opportunities I passed up because I

didn't think I was good enough and I didn't want to be ridiculed. I got enough ridicule at home; I was fat, I was nasty, I was lazy, I recall slouchy, oh and greedy, not to mention my butt was flat as a board. Those are just some of the toss arounds that I was characterized with when I was young. Now they weren't all labeled on me by my mom, I had a host of aunts, uncles, and cousins to heap up the negative adjectives. I'd learned after several years to guard my heart from the fun fest, but realized that in time it did affect me and the way I felt about myself. I (of course) blamed my mom for not beating up my aunts or defending me enough against the family's cruelty but she was also belittled frequently. That's just how it was in our family. It made me so mad that she would just brush things off and not allow them to upset her. I always thought when I get older I'm never going to let people talk to or about me harshly. I made a personal oath of immediate danger to any person who thought they could handle my children like I had been handled. I came out of the gate (adult life) with a chip on my shoulder after I realized I could actually fight a little bit. I just wanted a reason to unleash my furry on someone for the littlest thing. For a long time I had a plan to beat the living God out of my aunt Sandra as soon as I could take her. I remember she would do things like lock us in the bathroom when she baby sat us. She was just so dang mean! Now she is one of my favorite people to talk to in life and I love being in her company. It is funny how life teaches you to let go of the little things. On the flip side of that, some things are more difficult to release. I can truly laugh at these stories now, but growing up I couldn't because I had hurt feelings from them. I was so wounded and hurt by several things in my childhood. My Mom was a PYT (pretty young thing), so there was no shortage of fellas approaching her. Now don't get me wrong my mom wasn't just out there but I recall two guys from my early childhood. One married and one with a girlfriend that wasn't in the least bit afraid to sit on our porch with a shotgun. When I was seven my mom married my stepfather. Her requirement for him to have her hand in marriage was that he moved us from the projects that she also grew up in. He honored this request and purchased a house where we lived until I was 13. I assume it is evident that I kept a pretty long memory to recall boyfriends before the age of 7. I don't have the best of memories at all, so my conclusion is that certain things truly stick with us. I believe the reason I recall those things are that they were dramatic and there were other women involved. As I came of age and really understood those situations it made me look at my mother in a different way. My plan was that my children would never see me date until they were self-sufficient, if the marriage between their father and me didn't work out. I know a lot of people would disagree and that is absolutely OK because our differences are what make us all unique. I chose that route because the things I witnessed are etched in my mind in a way that I wouldn't want in my children's memory bank. I have made enough mistakes that they can judge me on, just from being a 17-year-old mom, so I treaded lightly. My mother's first husband was a womanizer, drunk, and an abuser. While he was a horrible husband to my mother, in my opinion, he respected his boundaries as a stepfather. I would have to seriously do something wrong for him to redirect me. He respected and understood that he didn't have to come in and play daddy. He worked and paid the bills but my mom worked also. I remember a time or two my mom had to go pick him up after a night of drinking and being robbed by prostitutes. On a rough night, he might come home and beat my mom because he felt like it. I remember on several occasions that I would get knives to defend my mom. Other times, I would just ram charge him so that the both of us could get the upper hand and beat him. This was at least a weekly or biweekly routine; it became a bit of a sport to me. I remember being sleepy for school the next morning after a night of fighting. On the other hand, I remember him cooking great Sunday dinners with domino games and lots of friends over. I remember him laughing with me and making funny jokes. I called him Poppa and without a doubt he loved me. He loved my mom too but it was a toxic kind of love. Obviously, he was a man with some serious soul wounds because there were spirits inside of him that were in rage. He was flawed in so many ways, as all of us are, but he was good to me as a step- father and I loved him. After several years, to no surprise, my mother left Poppa and the saga of my distain towards her deepened. Prior to the divorce my mother begun dating again. I am a firm believer in the principle that God is not going to bless your mess. In other words, it is my opinion that a marriage with a mistress from your first marriage is likely not going to work. Again, that is simply my opinion and I have no foundation other than my gut feeling on that matter. That brings us to a new chapter of my life that had almost detrimental effects on me at the time. When I was 13 my mother finally decided to leave Poppa. She had been wooed by her second husband who also had a girlfriend at the time. Now it didn't seem quite so odd to me at the time but again, as we come of age things get a bit more clear. Her second husband well that's just what I called him, my momma's husband. I felt that when he came along all stability, or what I knew it to be, was gone. I had to move in with my grandma because they could only afford a one bedroom apartment or something. I would sleepover over on the weekends and go swimming. My mom would come by pretty much every day after work, I'm not quite sure what for because I don't recall her cooking or helping with homework. On second thought, I guess it was to see me because we'd been living together for the first 13 years of my life up to that point. There had been periods we were apart. Most summers I would go visit my dad in Tennessee, but my primary home was with my mom. I guess by now it is pretty obvious that I wasn't very fond of my mother's second husband. Once I was old enough to analyze the situation, I concluded that her relationship was a tradeoff for a stable home. Once I did move in with my mom again I remember moving to different apartments or rent homes a lot. I don't even recall living in one place for over a year. I remember once I heard her husband say, "I pay my rent on time every month and the one time I'm late they gone say something." I thought, well you are supposed to pay your rent on time every month and their job was to say something if you are in fact late. He was a comical guy by his misconception as to what was right and wrong. He had children who would come visit and that was definitely a challenge for me. I never had a problem sharing my things, but I respected the things I had in order to preserve the use of them. I learned that at an early age, I began to be a bit of a compulsive organizer. I hated to see the corners on the boxes of the board games torn, it drove me crazy. His children lived in the country and were so very different than what I was used to. My mother seemed so nurturing and sweet to his daughter. By this time I was a pretty independent strong willed young lady and it drove me crazy to see her be so tender to someone when I felt that she'd dealt so harshly with me. I was a very developed girl at a fairly early age, so I looked much older and experienced than I was. My mother's second husband drank at the time but not to the extent of Poppa. One night I was up late in the restroom where we lived in doing my hair for school the next day. He came in the bathroom behind me and hugged my waist and kissed my cheek, I smelled alcohol from his pores. I was never fond of him and although I was a bit uncomfortable by the hug, I charged that to the fact that I disliked him. I blew it off as no big deal. The next night he came home drunk again but this time I was already in bed. As I laid on my stomach sleeping he slipped his hand under my chest and began to squeeze my breast. I never felt so disgusted in my life! I jumped up and yelled for him to get off of me and out of my room. He was so drunk he stumbled right into their room and I just continued to scream until my mother came in my room. I told her what happened so she called him out to the living room and he said I must have been dreaming. I was furious because it was bad enough that it happened but then to lie, I didn't comprehend. I didn't sleep for several weeks after that and I was severely depressed. I remember my mom talking to our pastor and other religious people about what happened and they concluded that the devil came into my room and fondled me. Authorities were never called and I was told not to let my grandmother know what had happened because it would be blown out of proportion. As you might imagine, my relationship with my mother seriously declined after that. I felt I was trapped in a situation that I couldn't get help for or talk to anyone about besides a trusted few that prayed for me. I mean come on; no one called the police, child protective services or anything! It was a horrible situation for me to be in because my mother stayed with him after that. It wasn't public knowledge until a year or two later when he tried the same with my cousin that lived with us. When he did I told her that he touched me too and then the rest of the family knew my uncle lived out of town but I remember him being here and telling me that I could live with my grandmother again. I know that her husband left for some time after that but I don't know where he went to. I don't even recall at what point my mother decided to let him move back in. I'm sure that was the point that I moved with my grandmother yet again. The next few years of my life were kind of back and forth between living with my mom when they would break up then staying with my grandmother when he would come back. I'd lost so much respect for my mother at this point because I felt that she was the source of all my pain. There came a point that I finally told my father what happened because I just wanted to leave. I hated being there with my mom and the pedophile, plus my grandmother was no cup of honey to be around either. I remember always being happy at my dad's house. At that point in my father's life he was faced with all kinds of turmoil himself, so living with him wasn't an option. The situation with my mother's second husband is one of the most difficult pieces of the puzzle for which I had to forgive my mother. I felt that she'd simply put me on the back burner for her desire to be with this man. My junior year in high school my mom and I had one of our explosive blowouts over the silliest of things. I remember inviting a friend to sleep over at our apartment, and buying groceries for the weekend. I called my mom to bring something for dinner that night and I would pay her back. She said that she didn't have money so I asked to speak with my grandma or her husband so they could get it for me on their way home. She refused to let me speak to them for whatever reason and I was angry with her. There was a much older guy that I'd been talking to at the time and I called him to bring us food. He did and just as he pulled off my mother pulled up and all hell broke loose. Being a smart mouth sixteen-year-old that despised her mother, I had a few choice words about the fact that there wasn't food to begin with. I'd gone on about if she would be a mother and make sure there is dinner I wouldn't have had to buy food stamps to get food for my friend to sleep over. I must give a shout out to my sister that had to witness that horrible ordeal that night (love you T). The argument got heated and I was put out of the house that night. I called the guy back to pick me up and I took what I could bag to my friend's house. Her mom let me stay there a night or two then I went to live with my cousin and his girlfriend at the time. It was like a house party all the time. They were a young fly couple plus her sister and another cousin stayed there also. They got me school clothes, ensured I got to school and that I was taken care of. My mom and I didn't talk for a while, I don't really recall how long. I know that she paged me on my birthday because she'd gotten me a huge bouquet of balloons. As much as I thought I hated my mother when I got the balloons, I knew that I didn't. The party at my cousin's house quickly ended when we were raided by the San Antonio Police departments' DEA. So, I bagged up my belongings and went back to my grandmother's house. Believe it or not I was still attending school regularly in the midst of all these circumstances. That is one thing I do pride myself on; there are millions of people that have done much better than me under more extreme situations but I've learned to take credit any way it comes. I'd lost all logical caution with my life by the time I was 17. My cousin told me someone was going to kill me because I didn't have an off switch. I would walk into harm's way without second thought and I was prepared at all times to kill or be killed if necessary. It was a very strange incident that made me come to this realization. My oldest was barely one month old at the time. I'd asked my cousin to drive me to the mother's house of the same guy that got me food when I got kicked out. For reasons that are so insignificant I can't even remember them but I was very angry. Initially I just wanted to be heard, but then it happened. He touched me! Oh my goodness, no he didn't! Did he hit me? Not at all; however, he grabbed my arm to walk me to the car so we didn't argue and disrespect his mother's house. Now that I'm a mother I can see that but in that moment things went black. I maneuvered myself in such a way that I got loose. I began to unleash a barrage of blows to his face in combination with bobs and weaves. Oh it was a thing of beauty, if you are into boxing. Until he hit back, I didn't want to fight anymore; I had to cut him. I was prepared with a knife in my pocket just in case my fighting ability was a tad off that day. I began to chase him then his mother jumped in front of me. My cousin is screaming bloody murder because she sees him with a semi-automatic weapon headed for me. She said, "Let's go, let's go he has a gun!!" In that moment, I paused; not to turn and run or calm down I paused to put myself closer to the weapon and exclaimed that I would die fighting. What the hell was I thinking?! As all of this happened my one month old baby starts to cry in the back seat of the car and then it hit me. Hello, Earth to Rachelle! He may not have planned to shoot me, but a slip could've easily happened. In my ignorance and my anger I could have taken my daughters mother away. I was in complete opposition with myself. I loved that child and wanted to give her the best life possible, but that 13-year-old girl inside of me had the power to be a warrior in that moment.

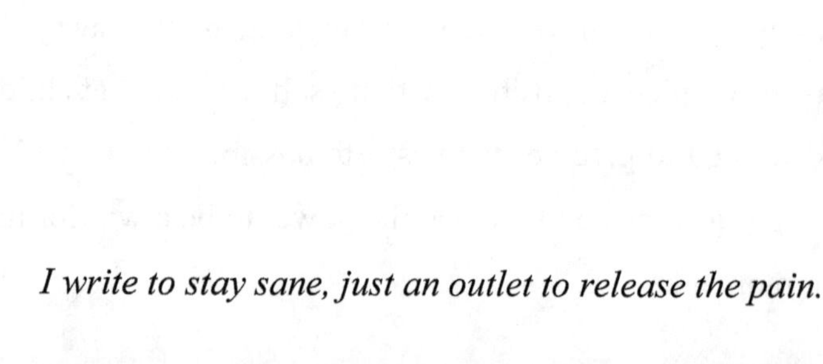

I write to stay sane, just an outlet to release the pain.

Every day I live, I live for someone else; I'm fighting all the pressures of hell by not killing myself. All my life I've been "loved" but not knowing how true. I've been unable to see past the hurt and that is blocking by who. Abandoned by my father, neglected by my mother, lead up to the end of being hurt by my lover. Who do I turn to when no one will listen? How can I find what I don't know is missing? Hiding behind a strength so false in deed, afraid to show my tattered soul in need. Rescue me Lord. Which way do I go? Heaven comfort me for my blessings will grow. These blessings I do love with all my heart but fear they too may tear it apart.

~Shel

Building Bridges

It never crossed my mind that God placed caretakers in my life. There was my cousin Julius, (who is the most maternal man I know) that babysat me a lot and changed my diapers. My aunt Doris was an angel, she would just let me be a big baby and love on me as much as I wanted. Not to mention those that provided food, clothes and shelter for me in times of need like my Grandma and my cousin Mike. I was surrounded by love that was rooted from my mother; specifically, my love from relatives. Along the years, I met and maintained friendships that are very significant to me. My friendships helped to provide the love and nurturing I felt I didn't receive from my mother. With the exception of one they are all females go figure.   I sought out other females that were overly affectionate and had an admiration for my quirky, yet flawed, individualism that I longed for. I'd characterized myself as the ugly duckling in my family, the fact that I was the only child (of my mother) that characterization should speak volumes. These friendships made me feel important and strengthened my self-esteem. To this day, I still have my circle of ten friends that I have known as far back as daycare and as late as high school that in some way or another know intricate details about me. I've been able to trust this group with my deepest pains and knew that their love and prayers covered my wounds. I have come to meet others that have become dear friends but I would be amiss not to mention the "Homies for Life." It is almost without fail that at some point or another they have individually impacted my life. Whether it was talking me down at a moment my anger took over, watching my children when I decided to go back to school, or just making me smile by sharing their world, my friends have truly been there for me. I think it is so important to surround one's self with positive people that motivate you to be a better you. I have friends that have degrees and some that finished high school later in life but when we are all together we are one people. We can look at each other through eyes of love not judgment so our differences add value to our relationships. That being said, I was very envious of some of my friend's mothers. Throughout our lives we have all learned to share the qualities of each other's mothers, mine included. For a long time I didn't see that as the blessing it was. Dark clouds of anger can truly suck the air out of every single positive thing in our lives.

The first time I looked at you and held you in my arms, I knew that I would love you my whole life long. I smile from your laughter, I cry from your pain. When all seems to fail you I will lighten your strain. God knows best the gifts bestowed, a truly remarkable blessing to watch you all grow. I will comfort you, protect you, do all that I can, I will teach you of life, for one day alone you must stand. You are my rocks and the reason I live every day, if ever harm were to haunt you my life I will pay. I vow now today and beyond whether I live or die God has made me the lucky one.

There is no me without you – Mommy.

~Shel

Motherhood

The preceding text is a poem I wrote as an optimistic new mother. I had plans in place to be the best Mommy I could be! Parenting is a tough job. It is by far the toughest I have faced in life and it can definitely leave a person drained. I couldn't allow myself to think that being a parent doesn't come with a manual. It was unthinkable for me to even consider that my mother had to learn as she went, just as I did. To even imagine the love that was shown by forfeiting her right to abort me was overwhelming. The sacrifices parents make on a daily basis was never considered when I thought of my mother. There were so many days I wish that I'd just been aborted or that I prayed for death of either of us to break free. The hatred and anger had grown so much that it took over the majority of my thoughts. It was like an infection that spread from my heart, then branched to my mind, and consumed my soul. I continued for several years to constantly critique my mother's parenting. I was 21 with three children and only a high school education. My husband worked and I stayed home with the children. We were on government aid and I felt that was good enough. I thought because I was making breakfast for my kids and I had no memory of my mom waking up early enough to make breakfast that I was a good mother. My frustration began to show up in the way I disciplined my children. It also showed in the way I handled situations in which I felt disrespected or victimized by someone else's actions. I remember being young and having the feeling that I just couldn't wait to grow up. At 13 years old, my son said the cutest thing to me one night as we were talking. He expressed to me that he wished he was young again. I thought really you are only 13 and you want to be younger than that. Then he went into more details; he said "I want to go back to the age where I don't have to clean my own throw up." I about died laughing! I remember when they were smaller I created this do everything, be everything superwoman image in my head. I felt guilty if I even had them do the most minor of things. In my head I would hear...you are just like your mom always wanting time to do what you want and your family needs you. I felt obligated to do it all and in time that obligation grew to frustration. I'd become so accustom to doing everything and when I was overwhelmed I wouldn't ask for help I would just explode. My children came to know a very strange imbalance in my personality because they were much too young to understand. My husband had come to a point of frustration as well because I was so unpredictable. All along I thought you know what I like (a clean house and structure) so just do that. I read somewhere that a service done without joy or expectancy doesn't help the servant or those being served. If I'm running around cleaning like crazy I don't want to see everyone lying around watching television. At the same token, I refused to say that we could get done faster if we all pitch in. It just didn't make sense to me that I had to ask for help. The children that I'd so delicately groomed to do what I needed them to do according to my preference weren't following suit. Go figure; our family doesn't just do what the heck we want them to do every minute of the day. I'm sure I didn't do everything they wanted me to do either. I felt because I worked hard to do all I was obligated to do that I deserved to have my other whims fulfilled. You know the queen of the castle that functions like a well-oiled machine. If I wanted my daughter to simply sit quiet like a princess, I shouldn't have had to ask at all but definitely not more than once. Then came my youngest, and oh my, she came on strong. Here was this child that went against every single rule my older two had easily settled into. This little tornado caused an uproar because now the other children think they should have an opinion as well. When my children came to the age of challenge I'd not anticipated it. I'd done everything "right" according to the rule book of mommy that only existed in my head! I was stern yet loving, supportive yet encouraged critical thought so they could be productive citizens. It didn't register that I had a philosophy of: please don't try to have too much individualism outside of my idea of the child I planned for you to be. What happened to me? I'd created a monster and had to pray for true patience as my children came of age. My reaction was to hit and yell or flex my power. The more I did those things, the less they responded. I was a big woman carrying the hurt and anger of a 13 year-old with the strength and voice to be reckoned with. I was ready to do or be damaged. In a moment that I praised my daughter for her character and for not being the typical teen that everyone speaks so harshly of, she reflected that I lived the example for her. In that instance, I realized that with all I'd done wrong and all the choices I could have thought through more, that I still touched her in a positive way. I had a WOW moment because, at that point I knew that my mother had many great qualities that touched me in a positive way also. She did in fact lay a mold for the hardworking woman I am today. There were certain things my mother wouldn't tolerate and other things I pushed the envelope on. One of the most valuable life lessons my mother instilled in me was that there were consequences for my actions. Like many mothers and daughters, there were times we disagreed but I give praise for the firm hand my mother had. I am definitely a more aggressive personality than my mother. I have now learned to appreciate the calmness in her that I once despised. There is a delicate balance between a mother and a daughter. I find that most women I've come in contact with are: just like, polar opposite, or some moderate variation of their mother's persona. Based on the stories up to this point, one can possibly guess that we are polar opposites. Oddly enough I don't believe that assumption is automatic. Many times we hate the things in others that we see in ourselves. One positive of the hardships my mother and I went through is that I learned from many of her choices. I felt that I lived only by my own will and the will of God and I never reflected that the most valuable thing my mother gave me was the belief in a higher power.

"Train up a child in the way he should go: and when he is old, he will not depart from it." (Proverbs 22:6 KJV)

I feel my responsibility for everyone else is making me irresponsible for myself. My efforts are sinking and even my health. No I can't read to you, clean the house and cook at the same time. Yet in this circle of life these chores are all mine. I chose to grow fast and travel this road. I find many treasures but I may have lost my soul. How do I cope Lord how do I climb? With no time for self, please help me survive. I offer my faith and you shall have my soul for this life you have given I relinquish control. Take me now your vessel to be used, no longer torn never again to be abused.

~Shel

Choosing to Break Free

After experiencing the failure of my super mom ego I expressed my heart in the preceding poem. I was far too ashamed to actually say that I didn't have this mother thing down like I thought. At about 25 years old I think the little girl in me decided to grow the hell up. I was tired! No really, I was sick and tired (no pun intended). Everything that was wrong in my life was my mother's fault! I was fat because my mom fried chicken; I was not as good in school as I could have been cause my mom wasn't supportive enough; I was a teen parent because my mom let me have too much free time. I took the car at 14 from church and hit a tree trunk; not to mention the time I got really drunk and threw up on her new carpet; oh and the skipped classes are a whole different story. Really!?! I mean the list goes on and on for things I would have sternly punished my kids for. As an adult, I reflected on some of the fore mentioned activities I took part in and I asked my mom if she thought I was a lost cause. She replied that she always knew I would be ok and I realized that her faith overruled my misconduct. Every failure or bad choice I'd made in my life I would justify it by the notion that I was doing better than my mom. I felt that as long as I was one step above my mother, I didn't have to succeed at anything else. What a huge mountain of denial I had to face and deal with. My mother put me in various activities when I was young to keep me active yet I had an insatiable appetite for the wrong things. My mother never suggested that I should have unprotected sex when I got pregnant. I never made an effort to be active or eat to healthy. Did my mother have faults? Absolutely. In fact, she made a lot of choices that, as a mother, I still can't make sense of. Does that mean that I had the right to go against the word of God "Children, obey your parents in the Lord for this is right" (Ephesians 6:1)? Absolutely not! Life is what it is and by definition that is "the animate existence of an individual." Notice how it doesn't specify that life is always good, or happy. It's just the damn existence which is what I found myself doing. I was surviving in my circumstances and holding myself captive by not allowing growth of my existence. I needed to grow my existence beyond just me, beyond my family and circle of ten. I needed to take all this bottled-up knowledge that I've acquired and share it with the world. I had to stop feeling sorry for me and start embracing my life lessons. If I continued to measure myself as one inch more than the efforts of my mother I would not meet my own potential. I would only be Carolyn's daughter, that wasn't just another statistic, but a statistic none the less. I believe that when individuals begin to accept responsibility for our own actions then we truly elevate as a people. When one takes time out to reflect on the choices that they've made and learn from them, they yield the best results for their future. It is critical that as we pass through time we evaluate ourselves, not harshly or critically but truthfully. There were so many times that I found myself making the same stupid choice or decision that I made in prior times. The results weren't exactly the same because I'd learned a little bit. However, the results definitely weren't positive. I'd began to make choices that were out right stupid, while anticipating a descent result.

I know where you've been, I can see where you're going. Let me guide you to the river with love overflowing. Honey child – that's what the old folks say – I can tell you a thing or two, about a thing or two that you can't see now but I have been through. Oh yes, I've been there down in despair searching for an answer that would never be there. Hoping, waiting, wanting then realizing! Yes, today God still works miracles the reality is they are sometimes worked through our choices. Hmmm…think about it; if I chose to allow the spirit to guide me past the valley through the anger, to the blessings he has been anxiously waiting to give…Oh what a miracle in this life of a wretch like me that has risen to be this sister of Christ. Take dominion over your eternity. Lose the bondage that has been embedded into your spirit, to curse your generations sanction over life and prosperity. Yes, you have that power because for now and forever more God's grace will remain to be AMAZING!!

~Shel

My Process

Even till this day I carry that same hatred of feeling like a victim of circumstance and unloved. This has manifested in a variety of ways in my life as situations would arise and I would grow angry or shut down. I, like so many others, am a work in progress and must allow myself grace to overcome negative emotions. I felt like "I'm not dead, in jail, or on drugs so I made it, I don't care about my past." I was wrong, I was terribly wrong. For many years, I battled my anger. I found myself handling situations that upset me in a manner that was not normal to my character. I was labeled as the girl that wore two faces. On one hand, I had so much love inside of me and on the other, I had a ball of anger that could leave my future in ashes. At some point in life I realized that I was very emotional. In fact, I would have reactions based on my feelings and sometimes those actions were negative. I had to learn that I couldn't make decisions based on temporary feelings that could lead to permanent negative effects in my life. As I grew beyond my emotions, I had the revelation that I was equipped as a child to be self-sufficient for a reason. There would be a time in my life that I needed my mother more than ever and life was preparing her for that time. There was a plan for me that I had no sight of and everything that I experienced was part of a process. Now I can live by the scripture "Honor thy mother that your days may be long on the land that the Lord God gives you." (Exodus 20:12) We never know what reaction may emerge from our action but we should damn sure prepare for anything. Does that mean going in blind to a situation? Definitely not! That means going into any situation expecting a variety of outcomes, some positive some negative. If we take time to think through our actions, we can visualize many resulting scenarios. After considering the results, we can make a well-rounded decision based on what's best for our situation. There are still times when I find myself in opposition with the better part of me, but I refuse to be labeled as "crazy". There are some things that are harder to deal with than others but that is what I'm working on. I never proclaimed that every action that I've taken is one of pride or the very best option I could choose. In fact, a few short years ago, I had a very violent reaction to my oldest daughter that could have ruined our relationship. I lost control of my emotions and I struck her in anger, to the point that I don't recall some of the incident. When the weight of what I'd done, regardless of my intent, hit me I hated myself. I took an action that has been passed down for generations that wasn't the best choice. By being completely realistic with myself and acknowledging my short comings I can continue to address them. One should not look to others to bring happiness because that is temporary. When the odds are stacked against us and we can't crack a smile through the tears, we have to depend on joy. I read somewhere that joy is the delight of the mind and happy is to be well adapted. What about when our adaptation has faltered? The things that at one point made us happy and we adapted to have changed. Where do you go when you no longer recall how to adjust to your circumstance? I guarantee it will not be in a mother, a child, a husband or a friend. When we find ourselves against a situation that looks ever more glum, we need to rely on our mind to reassure us of the blessings we do have. I truly know that trying to think of blessings in the midst of trials can be difficult, but it is not impossible. We have to realize that as long as there is air in our lungs, there is an opportunity to change our situation through spiritual guidance. It is such a relief when you take the time out to let go. It's, that simple. Just sigh and let go, understanding that things are not in our hands. Releasing that control just takes away that feeling of guilt and blame. I have been in situations where I felt that I had royally screwed up my life. I had to take a step back to admit when I didn't play a hand very well (made a bad choice). There aren't new cards but on the next hand I had to use a different strategy than before. I have to be realistic though, that is much easier said than done. I know people say you should forgive and forget but I learned that some things are never forgotten. Not to mention as we go through life we learn and identify things that we could have done differently. In February, 2011 I sat down again and talked with my mother about what happened with her second husband. When I told my mother what I experienced at that point in my life being 13 and afraid to sleep because of what happened, she had a completely different perspective of the situation. She felt that she'd handled the situation because it never happened to me again. She even asked why I didn't talk to her then and I had to remind her that at the time she didn't want to discuss it. I can truly say my mother is a different person today than she was then. I definitely don't agree with all the decisions she made in life yet I learned from each one. When my mother and I spoke, it was not to condemn her but I could definitely tell that she listened to me differently at 33, than she did when I was 13. When I forgave her husband, I released power into my life. I don't feel that is crying over spilled milk, I believe it is looking at a picture from a different angle. I can profess to the many challenges of womanhood and motherhood. Children are blank canvases when they are born. The art of mothering paints expectations and disciplines with care and affection. Children don't come with hand books and I am thankful for the art of my mother's parenting because ultimately it shaped me into the woman I am today.

I was your passage to life. I know no greater gift than you choosing me to manifest your glory through and allow me to mold you as your mother. My humility is great, my emotions are overwhelming, for you occupy my life in a way that only Gods can understand. Be who is within you to be and never allow failure to be your final destination.

~Mom

The variation in my poetry reflects the evolution of my belief system, to one of pure spirituality. I have built a legacy that is still under development. I had a conversation with my youngest daughter about being an "independent woman." I explained to her the difference that I see in that term versus what society may portray it to be. I recounted a time when her father was out of work for months so there was no child support coming into our household. As a planner, I relied on savings and tight budgeting for the most part, but there came a point where even that wasn't enough. I worked a second job for some time until their dad found work and could contribute again. I did that because as a mother I wanted to have stability for my children instead of uprooting them due to a tough situation. I wanted her to know that although I have the ability to support myself and children financially, that I still very much valued the partnership of a two-parent home. I took the time to explain that to my daughter because my concern is also for her future husband. I don't want my daughters and son to perceive that it is ok for women to be so hardened by society or the expectations we place on others, that we can't see the value that our male counterparts bring to our lives. There are so many aspects to life that can challenge your very will to live. Every situation, circumstance and challenge is a step toward your purposed path in life. Choose to make a difference in your own life before choosing to give up hope based on your circumstances.

In the winter months, open the window of your soul to the possibility of life in the form of purpose. Be an evolution of reality. In the absolute realm of life, close your eyes, seek guidance, be life, feel all, learn unceasingly and love infinitely.

~Shel

ABOUT THE AUTHOR

Rachell Hathaway was born and raised in San Antonio, Texas as an only child. After graduating high school she focused on being a mother and wife for many years before finally graduating in 2016 with a Bachelor's in Finance from the University of the Incarnate Word. She is currently pursuing her Master's Degree in Public Relations at the University of Texas at San Antonio, while working in Community Relations for one of the world's leading financial institutions.

Email her at rshel77@icloud.com

Her website is www.shelhathaway.com